ITS OWN PLACE

poems of faith and spirituality

Marion Bond

MARION BOND

First published in Great Britain in 2016

Dixon-Stuart Books
3 The Soke, Alresford
Hampshire SO24 9DB

ISBN 978-0-9934358-4-3

Printed and bound in Great Britain by Sarsen Press, Winchester

Marion Bond was born in Dumbarton, in 1955 and subsequently attended The University of Glasgow, where she studied English Language and Literature.

The next three and a half decades were spent in teaching English at independent and comprehensive schools and Sixth Form colleges, in Glasgow, Yorkshire and Hampshire.

Successful in international poetry competitions, including the University of Southampton International Writers Conference and the Wells Festival of Literature and a reviewer for poetry magazines, such as South, she has performed her work alongside Ruth Padel, Don Paterson, Chris Logue, Jo Shapcott and Wendy Cope at venues as diverse as The Edinburgh Fringe, The Gantry, The New Forest Arts Centre and Winchester Cathedral.

The mind is its own place, and in itself

Can make a heaven of hell, a hell of heaven

John Milton: Paradise Lost Book 1 lines 254-255

... Nor in this bower,

This little lime-tree bower, have I not mark'd

Much that hath sooth'd me…

No plot so narrow…

No waste so vacant, but may well employ

Each faculty of sense, and keep the heart

Awake to Love and Beauty!

S T Coleridge: This Lime-Tree Bower My Prison

CONTENTS

Preface

The poems in *Its Own Place* are published for the first time in this collection, though all of them have appeared in poetry magazines, or online. Some date to the late 1990s, when I used to successfully enter international competitions, such as the poetry section of the Wells Literary Festival, where I was awarded First Prize by the novelist, Helen Dunmore.

I suppose that I need to supply a preface, though, like Wordsworth - and this might be my only connection - *I could declare: I never cared a straw about theory.* However, this would not be strictly true, in my case at least, as I was privileged to study Literary Theory under that colossus, Philip Hobsbaum.

Pondering on the relation of poetry to life itself, I aspire to the endeavour of the Romantic Poets, who intended to present a selection of language spoken in a state of *vivid sensation.*

It is the prerogative of the reader to ascertain whether I have afforded the emotional moment sufficient time and space for tranquil recollection.

As Coleridge put it in his *Biographica Literaria*, I hope that I have *rescued the most admitted truths from the impotence caused by the very circumstances of their universal admission.*

Musing on myth, place and childhood, many of my poems are written in the first person, but in the guise of various personae.

I favour blank verse for its conversational and versatile qualities and I experiment with forms, such as the sestina and the villanelle.

Perhaps a certain unease with post-Reformation individualism led me to modify my preoccupation with all things intellectual and cerebral and led me to an engagement and relationship with the gentler influences of Fancy, or the Imagination and its uplifting zephyrs of transportation.

The lime-tree bower, though a kind of prison, was no restrainer of liberty for an abandoned Coleridge. He was able to join his wandering friends in their exploration of Nature, though he was physically constrained at Nether Stowey.

Many writers have experienced liberation through exercising the faculty of Fancy. John Bunyan and Paul, the Apostle, spring to mind immediately.

I trust that the reader of this modest first collection will be able to join me in my aspiration to:

...gaze till all doth seem

Less gross than bodily; and [observe] such hues

As veil the Almighty Spirit, when yet he makes

Spirits perceive his presence…

To catch a fleeting glimpse of:

…the slip of smooth clear blue betwixt two Isles

*Of purple shadow…**

might make our engagement all too worthwhile.

**Coleridge: This Lime-Tree Bower My Prison*

Marion Bond, 2016

AGNOSTICISM

All his life the sinner cried:

Ah dinna ken; Ah dinna ken.

And when he died, he cried,

Ah didna ken; Ah didna ken.

And the de'il replied,

Weel, ye ken noo.

PELERIN

I carried our sins all the way, coquette,
my calloused heels crushing cackling demons
and saw the face of Christ radiating
from each basin-bearing hospitaller.
I beat back hell-hounds in every hameau,
with my bog oak staff, my waisted gourd poured
down a parchment throat, as parched as the paths
I'd traversed to totter on that jetty.
Discarded oyster shells scarified soles,
as I scrambled onto the final ship
and I tried to erase your siren face
which haunted me from corbels, chevets
and polychromatic stone caskets,
from Aulnay, Saintes - and even Talmont.
Over the glittering estuary,
the Damascene sun glared epiphany.

Host fragments on my tongue, salt tang on teeth,
I'd hoped that the next kiss of a chalice

would transport me home, with my talisman:

a stringed scallop, showing where I had been.

Then I scattered blood-red hollyhock seeds,

like blisters, into the wake, trusting that

each would burst into a pillar of fire,

to illuminate my return voyage.

I would walk over waves, though I was lame;

I'd wrestle with archangels, tear my nails

on all those petrified palmers' handprints,

into which I'd press my desperation.

From Santiago I would come, burning,

like a bush that could never be consumed:

shriven, forgiven, ready for Heaven.

Now you too must go beyond the Gironde.

(Talmont, on the Gironde estuary, was an important stop for pilgrims in the Middle Ages. They received communion at the church of St Radegonde before setting sail for Santiago de Compostela.)

ANOTHER LOOK AT THE ARUNDEL TOMB

I might have known
the tender clasp
evoking the tension
between Time and Love
(symbol of faithfulness)
is possibly a nineteenth century
addition, a terminal inexactitude.
But is it?
Now it's thought to be original;
its loyalty as genuine
as the little dogs under their feet.
I might have known
Larkin's best phrase:
final blazon
was Monica's invention,
replacing his weak *signal.*

I might have known
Arundel Tomb isn't a grave.

It’s in Chichester

and is a memorial,

strictly speaking.

The Fitzalans are buried

in Lewes Priory,

to be precise.

So, what is truth?

Maybe we should all cross our fingers

and hope that we can make it work.

Eleanor crossed her legs

and yet seemed to make

the public presentation

more than acceptable.

Nothing is written in stone.

VIEWING THE TADDEI TONDO

It's obvious half realisation
is more fascinating, enigmatic,
than bold, bezelled actualisation.
We've climbed vitreous steps, automatic
in our assumption they will bear our weight,
and now stand face to face with Christ, St. John.
The babe recoils from His prefigured fate.
A goldfinch holds their - and our - attention.
This is that same bird whose blasphemous theft
of berries from Messiah's thorny crown
drew scarlet beads from His brow: all this left
to our imagination and not shown -
a veil not dragged right back, but partly drawn.
And marble's own epiphany, éclat,
provides the nimbus we rely upon,
hallowing all with a magnificat.

We seem to stand upon mere reflection,
art aiding in us the visionary;

summoning faith in His resurrection:
elevation from the ordinary.
Our souls are gradually teased, released,
as we feel translucence behind stone's chill.
In a blink we find wonders haven't ceased
and the master chisel is not yet still.
Like struggling slave figures in Florence,
who grapple to achieve transformation
from half-hewn blocks, seeking deliverance,
our striving eases in adoration.
Contemplating heaven with feet of clay,
we find relief; moulds break and fall away.

(Michelangelo Buonarroti, the Royal Academy. In Christian iconography, the goldfinch symbolises the Passion and is an emblem of endurance and fruitfulness).

THE TENDERNESS OF STONE

We know beggars would rather have a loaf
so, when they cry, they do not want a stone.
Too long a sacrifice can turn a heart
into one of us, as can persistence.
Children will skim us time and time again
over a still loch and troubled adults
will cast us out as far as they can see,
to drown their burdens, like a sack of cats.
We are chips off the old slab, rocks, boulders,
pebbles, grains, irritants that create pearls.
We have been molten, crystallized, polished;
we have been dragged, eroded, scarified.
Attrition has been our second nature.
We have fissures, fossils, fool's gold, dark seams.

Look at us: though we have been rejected,
we also have been chosen corner stones,
cairns, sheepfolds. Hollowed out, we became homes.
Thirsty crows dropped us, one by one, until

the water level rose to meet their beaks.
We have been used as missiles to kill men - projectiles
of their own guilt. But one Man
made a mad crowd release us to the ground,
rather than hurl us with the force of law.
We have borne words and cryptic alphabets;
we have been pillows, then piled as pillars
to mark the place where angels ascended,
descended on a heavenly ladder.
We mark time, are thresholds, lintels and sills.
Some implore that we should fall upon them;
some sense that they should fall on us and break.

We are the worn handclasp of effigies
and the spray of gravel at a shutter;
the shrapnel signal of elopers' trysts.
The mobile statue of the petrified,
whom faithless men implore to punish them,
finds in rapprochement there's no rebuke.

In a future world the shattered will cup

palms, to receive a stone, white as an egg,

bearing their new name. And stones will not chide.

Heaven will be in every grain of sand.

EASTER 1996

That week we ventured outside at midnight,
when a shadow gradually snuffed the moon,
till the reddened orb, deprived of its light,
stared like the Baptist's eyeball. In high noon
we think the spotted sphere no longer there.
All the primitive tribes rise to my mind,
who must have viewed such an eclipse, despair
weighing stricken hearts. How they must have signed
to each other when they became aware
of its reappearance. So a small group
watched the waning of their Son as darkness
covered the earth, but they were to recoup
The Light of the World. This Easter I bless
the God of Heaven for resurrection,
looking to the sky for inspiration
through my cataract eyes. So inspection
of the new moon tends to celebration.
Astrological symbols directed
men to the babe. Lunar allegory,

which by most people would be rejected,
confirms for me the Good Friday story.
Most of the time I look through the wrong end
of the telescope; get a false picture;
let the neon town lights obscure my Friend;
forget He's an omnipresent fixture.
He who controls the weather, cycles, tides,
is sometimes indiscernible through cloud;
never disappears, though He sometimes hides:
rises like Lazarus minus his shroud.

EULOGY

Pontius Pilate played under your branches
in Fortingall, it's alleged, two thousand
years ago, before he would wash his hands
of Innocence. Crimson shells of arils
broke out like bloodbeads on a thorned brow
and he trod on golden prickles, so sharp
they pierced his sandals. Rootstock of saplings
for a future planting, you are much more
than three-in-one. Funeral corteges
passed through your hollow trunk, more easily
than camels through the eye of a needle.
Later young men trimmed your boughs for longbows.
Ancient churchyard trees abutting the butts
united sacred and secular. In this space,
one rootball bound the dead
of the parish in a communal grave.

Portions of this yew may have been a man
the Governor knew. *Memento mori*;

toxic and taxil, your lost heartwood rings
defy establishment of your true age.
Christian evergreen? Druidic icon?
You were a linchpin of society
by the lychgate of a newly planted church.
You may stand here when certainties are gone.

MIRACLE IN MUCH MARCLE

It's Good Friday: we are driving eastwards
through drifted fields, where ewes have lost their lambs.
Arriving early at the church, its latch
gives mercifully and so we enter,
stumbling into a chancel of pure light.
Attention is diverted to others
who lie in a petrified majesty:
a metaphysical conceit in stone.
Where is the wimpled beauty, tight-buttoned
sleeve? We want to gaze on serene eyelids.
We'd like to witness Jairus' daughter
miraculously wake before the end
of Time. This childless spouse, unknown daughter,
took to sleep, shutting out her father's death
at Tyburn; his treachery with a queen;
his complicity in vile regicide.
Unprepared for absence's disclosure,
we're disappointed - not as disciples
who found a luminescent gardener.

There's no grave mole-catcher to interview.
She has risen; there has been a Rapture.
We see that her heraldic tomb has gone
in the twinkling of an eye and no cloth,
no folded linen's there - just vacancy,
where Blanche, her sins as white as snowy wool,
blank as a virgin, slept in innocence.
We read she has gone for restoration;
but surmise transfiguration took place
almost a millennium ago.
Centuries have tolled through her long fingers,
each bead once a prayer for deliverance:
for ours; not hers, that having been achieved.

THE FORGIVENESS WINDOW

This was to have been a thirteenth blind pane,

seen only from the outside of the church:

replacement for its bombshell-slivered glass.

Judas, the betrayer, hangs from a tree.

His grasp relaxes and thirty pieces

of silver metamorphose into a

c

a

t

a

r

a

c

t

of flowers.

Discernment can come from outside the Church.

Inside some, coin-lidded, opt for cataracts.

Most see through glass darkly; few face to face.

(Engraved for Moreton Church, Dorset, by L. Whistler. Now received into the church, after having been stored for years in the Dorchester Museum).

THE JUDAS TREE

Those plumb-like seed pods cannot mask the corpse.
The sagging branch touches the earth. Strange fruit
suspended from a limb: a pendulum
measuring a moment of treachery.
At each bloom's heart is a crown of thorns.
From the scarified trunk blood beads burst forth -
a rosary protecting its blush of shame.

Cybore had a premonition:
she dreamt her son would ruin Issachar.
She and her husband, Ruben, cast him off -
Moses-like, adrift, in a pitched basket.
He then washed up on Scariot, whose Queen,
childless, lonely, feigned a pregnancy,
taking the outcast child to her own breast.

Anxiety dispelled, she then conceived
her own son, Jacobus, whom Judas loathed.
Supplanted, he destroyed, as Cain did; fled
to Pilate's service in Jerusalem.
Then, asked to fetch his master some ripe fruit,
he argued with the owner of the land
and slew him with a rock. Haceldama -
The Field of Blood - is his, with the man's wife,
who promptly tells him of his parricide.
Now he is Sicarius: *assassin.*

He follows Jesus, seeking redemption,
yet dips his fingers in the common purse
and, angry that three hundred silver coins
spent on some precious ointment should be poured
on the Messiah's feet, he takes umbrage;
betrays his Master for a tenth of that -
the price one paid to liberate a slave.

Since bowels of mercy he had none, he spilt
his innards from that tree, so that his soul's

quietus should not defile the lips
that had kissed God. He died not on the earth;
nor in the heavens, where men and angels range,
but dangled in the air, devils' plaything.

Jesus harrowed Hell to plant His tree:
to cut down Judas and to set him free.
Look! Now we see the pods have seeds in them
and, though deciduous, those leaves return,
heart-shaped, assuring us of sins forgiven.
Its branches lifted up, like hands in prayer,
surrounded by an intense cloud of nard,
the Redbud props a ladder to the stars
and even men like Judas can aspire
to Paradise, via The Tree of Life.

Blood-geld bought the Gentile burial plot -
the first Garden of Rest, that Potter's Field.
(Sanhedrin-laundered guilt's slick charity.)
But the Potter makes new vessels from shards,
firing up His kiln from the Joshua trees.

ALL SAINTS' CHURCH, STEEP - GOOD FRIDAY

It is steep, but we find it after all,
with memorial tablet on the wall,
listing old choirboys - Cranstone, Applebee,
whose treble piping trills continually
in shrill birdsong. Death's head kneelers proclaim
memento mori. We don't forget name,
or words from the believer whose etched glass
invites us to see less darkly; to pass
through the pain, through the pane, beyond the moss
of an Easter garden, with central cross,
till our gaze follows glaze to Downs and sky,
clouded momentarily by the sigh
of some Hampshire widow, for whom the coat
on washing line; the unsmoked pipe denote
an absent man and yet a spirit nigh,
the daffodils bugling in Reveille.

PINTOR DEL REY

His enigmas of dark bodegas where
every week is Semana Santa and
humble figures poach eggs; serve their fellows;
wait for a sharp sunbeam epiphany;
show more intensity than a brazen gleam
from mortars, or a water droplet's sheen.
Dim Seville interiors, shaft-denied,
divulge a dignified resignation
to the present; trust that significance
may dawn. Unspoken communication
resonates with diverse shared agendas.
Glaucous fish eyes uncomprehendingly
stare in Martha's kitchen, but through the hatch
is glimpsed the divine. That young mulatto
girl, washing up, is suddenly aware
of a moment of grace in her tavern:
an Emmaus experience. The boy,
who so anxiously clutches a trussed melon
quadranted by a knotted, twisted cord,

seems to sense he cradles a wounded world,

whose riches are bound up and can't be shared - yet.

As he receives cool water, a man's face,

mystery-shrouded, looks on silently.

Is he the fourth man, the one from the den?

Is he aware that the same boy's destiny

will be to attend the Adoration

and possibly witness the death of God?

In the event of a resurrection,

will someone dare to open the shutters

and let the sun tear through the curtained shroud?

(An Old Woman Cooking Eggs, 1618, Velazquez, Scottish National Gallery)

POEM FOR JENNY

…who died in the 7/7 London bombings, 2005

The Deplorable Word was uttered
some time around nine o'clock that morning.
The girl had just been reading about it -
how witch Jadis 'owned' the people of Charn,
though *her* powers did not work in England.
Then the girl must have touched the magic ring,
for suddenly the prequel of her life
ceased and she was translated to a wood
between multiverses. Her watch then stopped.
And, not having the two green rings with her,
she couldn't return.
She thought she could hear a low, growling sound,
not threatening; quite musical, really:
nothing like the noise of the Underground.
She was looking down at the Tube carriage;
she was looking down now on the carnage.
Someone was using her book to prop up
a stranger's head. She was glad they took it.

She had no use for it now, but she knew
she was a protagonist in its plot.
Those pages would never close; her story
would continue, not in allegory,
but as a dark, complicating event,
part of the concatenation before
the revelatory denouement.
Some worlds begin and others end like this:
not with a bang and a whimper of pain,
but with a story that can't be untold;
part of the greatest narrative ever.
She looked into a pool and was surprised
to see the reflection of a lion
in a tranquil surface, with no shock waves.
The music seemed to emanate from him.
In the beginning was his word
and now she knew he would have the last one.

ST PETER'S FISH

We had toiled till daybreak and caught nothing,
trawling mercury stains on the glass lake,
but finding them fishless. He stood watching
us: fishers of men, breathless, scarce awake,
with calloused hands. Though His breath caused the world
to emerge, He gave us no assistance.
Perhaps the sight of our washed nets unfurled -
co-operation and sheer persistence -
showed Him fallen men performed some tasks well.
When we'd exhausted our efforts, He said:
Try the other side of the boat. I tell
you, prophesy that a multitude fed
on two fish is nothing to me. Vast draughts,
miraculous ingatherings await you.
Much later, on the shore, we spied a waft
of smoke and smelt some broiling fish. He cooked
our breakfast. We marvelled and ate.
He joined us: a fish out of water; looked
the same, drawing His symbol on the sand.

I dredged my mind to find inspiration
to write about Him, but was barren and
no silver flickerings of creation
took my bait. Then He blew on smoking coals,
which I kissed. Their heat took me to my cross,
but not before I'd netted many shoals
of men, small fry and large, for His great cause.

JACOB'S WELL

They labelled me: *The Woman at the Well -*
Put in the Pitcher by a Nazarene!
They said I had a story that would sell.

Swine rooted round me, snuffling at the smell
of scandal - reckless as those Gadarene.
They labelled me: *The Woman at the Well…*

and camped outside my house, convinced I'd tell;
amazed that He should speak to the unclean
and said I had a story that would sell.

Some vowed He'd mesmerised me; cast a spell
on me; elaborated what they'd seen.
They labelled me: *The Woman at the Well…*

Those paparazzi made my life sheer hell.
Why not take the shekels and spill the beans?
They said I had a story they could sell.

Rabboni's Living Water seemed to quell

my raging thirst. Now I know what peace means.

They labelled me: *The Woman at the Well*

*Who had a Story that She Wouldn't F***ing Sell!*

KILLED BY KINDNESS

The Fatted Calf speaks:

No, the Golden Calf was a relation,
but nobody bows down, or worships me.
I've been a long time in the fattening,
unlike those who claim, *I don't eat that much*,
but who keep piling on pound after pound -
or should I say minas, pims and bekahs?
I've been stuffed to the gunnels and force-fed
over a fairly lengthy period:
I'd say since about the time the boy left.
Every day his father filled my manger;
he'd talk to me while tears coursed down his cheeks.
The elder son, the one who was jealous,
thought he'd sink his teeth into me one day -
maybe as the main course at his wedding,
but none of the girls like his attitude.
He still has a mother to care for him,
though she keeps comfort eating all day long.
But my old Ma was sold off long ago

and my younger brother was sacrificed.
I've felt separation anxiety!

Apparently, he was living it up
on some all-expenses paid gap year.
Now his mamma regrets ever nagging:
Tidy your room. It looks like a pig sty!
The gossip is he's had to take a job:
Trust Fund Kid is working as a swineherd.
The Bank of Dad is into overdraft.
Son's discovered he can't make a silk purse
out of a sow's ear. Enough is a trough.
He's never going to bring home the bacon.
But at least his porcine companions
don't wallow like humans in self-pity.
In our own ways, we're confined to our stalls -
unless he swallows his pride and comes home.
Meanwhile I'm feeling about to explode.
The elder son is imprisoned too.
His father confines himself to the farm,
not socialising, lest his son should call.

You could say I'm being killed by kindness
and maybe the boy feels that he was too.
Lord knows, he was a party animal,
but we could all do with some cheering now.

BETHESDA MIRACLE

Dumped by my friends, yet again, at the pool -
the same boring view for thirty eight years.
Occasionally some ripples stirred:
phantom movements of an angel?
But, unlike others, I couldn't move,
so Passover was a pun on my life.

I had a lame excuse for my sad life.
I'd always lost in Life's lottery pool.
And, when those ripples began to move,
the lucky ones, in former years,
would jump in; tried to swim to the angel.
Over The Five Porches, the rock doves stirred.

The others were stir crazy. I never stirred -
until I had the Shabbat of my life.
A man, not in the guise of an angel:
a stranger, wandered round the pool,
looking younger than the thirty eight years
I had lain there. He told me to move.

Surely he could see my wasted limbs? *Move!*
Yet the first odd fluttering of hope stirred
my paralysed frame of thirty eight years.
Was this some seraphic Prince-of-Life type
manifesting himself at a sheep pool?
Why choose me? God knows I was no angel.

Friends had stopped believing in the angel.
They had moved on; but I couldn't move.
I became their social burden, the pool
a place of mutual respite. I'd be stirred
from sleep; they'd dress me (altruism's life-
long sentence). The same routine for years.

Why did I hang on to life for years,
when anyone could see that the angel
had decreed my miserable life
was not such as would move
any heavenly being to be stirred
to transform me, at home, or at the pool?

For years I've helped others move to the pool.

Stirred by gratitude; given back my life:

I never doubted that he'd been the angel.

THE MIRACULOUS BEAM

I

Someone was trying to tell us something,
the project manager, Flambard, declared.
When we attempted to lay foundations
at St Catherine's Hill, the materials
went missing; re-appeared two miles away.
So, we returned to the old Saxon site.
Still the stuff disappeared into thin air.

II

Aye, sighed the Master Quarryman, *you'll find*
there's always someone cutting corners;
taking home off-cuts to please his missus,
who wants some extra shelves above her fire;
a new table; rockers for a cradle.
And now the gaffer is going to find out
because the board-hewer claims that the joist
is shorter than it was the night before.
And when we tried to hoist it into place
it didn't fit the specification.

III

The chippie with the enigmatic smile -
always the last to knock off on Fridays,
had worked through his lunch-breaks and took no pay.
When brawls broke out with the apprentices,
he'd mutter something about motes and beams,
continuing to plane with his scarred hands:
a halo of sawdust gilding his head.
He said he'd get his father to help out,
as if something which fell short could be fixed.

IV

He set The Seven Stars, he re-joindered.
Pub refurbs are not the same thing, they quipped.
The night is coming when no man can work,
So, talking of pubs, we're heading there now.
No man builds without calculation.
We've heard that one before, the masons laughed.
He drew a circle on the tracing floor.
Who does he think he is? They quaffed their ale.
Perhaps Architect of the Universe!

Flambard's coming round tomorrow first thing.

A happy bunny he's not going to be.

The whole roof could cave in at any time.

Frankly, we could do with a miracle.

V

Flambard – who can see angels on pinheads -

gazes up from the ambulatory.

The beam that the builders had rejected

is now integral to the whole building.

We've heard of the budding of Aaron's staff,

but this is something else, the guildsmen laugh.

VI

But the carpenter with the quizzical face -

Not a trace of him was ever found,

save for the load-bearing tree in its place

and the print of his sandal on the ground.

(inspired by a visit to Christchurch Priory, where one can still see the beam, located in the Priory's Ambulatory).

SCHUBERT IN SALISBURY

Our invisible feet traverse The Close
and we are shrouded in darkness. It's there:
luminous, transcendent, yet immanent,
its sculpted details sharp in the moonlight.
Together, on this frosty evening,
our hearts ache from Schubert's yearning lieder:
betrayal, grief, regret and bitterness.
Oh, farewell to the world - let them feel love;
they may thank you yet - sooner or later,
but tearfully - and probably too late.
In the medieval hall she sang to us
and we were insulated by the warmth,
the spotlit dais, the shiny Steinway.
Elbow to elbow, we brushed each other;
applauded to show solidarity.
But, propped up, in the great closed porch, a lone
cold, shadowy figure, tightly cocooned
in damp, lumpy bedding, breathes not a word.
The stone finger of God points to the sky,

as if to seal the lips of the Divine.
Before us lies a man who has no voice,
but merely craves some heat from God's stage door.
The singer did not bow to him tonight;
he did not hear the piano lid come down.
He falls asleep and hears the angels sing -
the spire above, his ladder up to Heaven.
And we, like Jacob, rooted to the earth,
wrestle and wrestle with our own demons.
The moon vanishes behind a dark cloud.
She sang: *Und finster die Nacht, wie das Grab!**
The frozen sleeper turns onto his side
and we hurry, before the gates are locked.

**and the night dark as the grave.*

STABAT MATER

This masonry should cry aloud to hear
the validation of the Virgin's pain.
The distillation of a single tear
incorporated in the sad refrain:
O quam tristis et afflicta…

Theorbo and bass viol underpin
the strings' and singers' interplay,
as Pergolesi paints for us the price of sin
and strips the intervening years away.
Crucifixi fige plagas…

I look around to where an honoured few
unite to share the Mother's anguished strain,
participate in passion from the pew,
reflecting that her loss became their gain.
Fac me vere tecum flere.

Yet those outside are steeped in disregard:
the congregation numbers twenty two.
The music scents the church as spikenard,
an alabaster jar shattered anew.
Cruc hac inebriari.

Writhing in time with the continuo's pace,
a household fly performs its deathly dance.
Oblivion meets its fate and yet I face
a fact imbued with strange significance.
Quando corpus morietur fac ut anime donetur…

We leave the haven of this ark
to find no armistice has been declared
and slip into the graveyard's cloying dark.
As prey in evil's web we seem ensnared.
Fac me cruce custodiri morte Christe premuniri - confoveri gratia.

The music of the spheres has set that fly;

in memory's amber it will resonate.

Transfiguration gild us as we die;

such harmony our end alleviate.

Amen.

(inspired by a performance on Mother's Day, 1993 in Meanwood, Leeds)

ON HEARING MY FIRST CUCKOO IN SPRING

Two notes transported me to Picardy,
for this birdcall, with its insistency
was a clarinet conceptualised
by a syphilitic man, who, near-blind,
was propped in his wheelchair in Grez-sur-Loing.
His Gaugin *Nevermore* had then been sold;
Grieg's Scandinavian scenery mere
pointillist impressions. Now sound was all -
the lapping of the river at the end
of his garden; his giggle at the church
when he broke out at his confirmation;
the rhythms of his poet friend, Verlaine;
those haunting spirituals he'd overheard
through the cigarillo smoke in Solano,
when the grove could have been a kind of grave;
Grainger's laugh; Heseltine's accusation;
Fenby's chords; a populous city's noise;
the barking of the dachshund he once gave
to a favourite sister those years ago;

the rustle of his father's Yorkshire Post:

I see that Fritz has given a concert;

the sound of spiteful stones smashing shutters

and soldiers' boots searching out their wine hoard.

In the New Year they made his cuckoo sing,

but by Autumn it sang over his plot,

laurel-lined in Lingfield. Jelka heard it,

tumour-riddled, from the nursing home.

That day they sent her a boxed-set greeting

on a gramophone recording, but found

she'd already heard it; flown to meet him.

Now as I walk along this river bank,

the trite threnody does not interrupt

the inexorable ongoing flow

of Life itself. This is what makes us rapt:

what Delius sensed, and helped us to know -

that two notes must not usurp the whole scale.

EIN DEUTSCHES REQUIEM FÜR D-DAY

The breath of that great soul speaks in hushed tones,
soothing survivors of Allied assaults -
Brahms bathing the buttered Normandy stones:
tinting kaleidoscopic windows. Vaults,
in cross-ribs, soar to swelling resonance;
reverberate sharp reminiscences
of those who suffered in this audience.
Choral voices soften dissonances.
Ja, der Geist spricht. No permanent abode
can house indomitable souls on earth.
When Destruction came, still sweet music flowed,
inspiring creativity where dearth
had reigned before. The youthful soldiers sleep,
lullabied to lilt of liberation:
seeds watered by grief of those who now weep.

They've passed beyond that twinkling of an eye
and rest, sung heroes. Heartfelt ovation
from grateful present shows they'll never die
in memory, or appreciation.
And when that final bugle sounds, they'll rise,
as one, not knowing discrimination,
to jointly celebrate War's own demise.

(inspired by a choral performance in Lisieux Cathedral)

THE SYCAMORE SINGS

Shall life renew these bodies? Of a truth

All death will he annul…

(amended words from his poetry on Wilfred Owen's gravestone)

Where his mother muted her offspring's ire,
deleting his line's interrogative;
where Dufay scored his music at Cambrai;
St Quentin's corpse loomed from the Somme marshland,
to hallow the grandest basilica;
where guillotines did their grisly work,
fog lifted from shattered Bois l'Eveque -
new dawn drawing back night's curtain of war.

On a towpath, a twenty five year old,
tried not to fret how he would cross the bridge.
Mesmerised by the autorotation
of seeds, he foresaw his own slow spiral,
where magpies croaked in blasted canopies.
Dark, stark poplars had been lopped long before;
the copses razed; the rides and lynchets scarred.

Mametz, Maricourt and Bois des Fourcaux:
sweet chestnut, lime, beech, hazel, oak, hornbeam -
mad mandrakes uprooted; bi-furcated trunks.
Sad remblais of Hebuterne (No Man's Land)
absorbed shrill batteries near sunken lanes.
Calvaires bowed before continuous suffering.

In Beaumont Hamel, a single tree remains,
petrified. In Delville Wood, The Last Tree
stands like a gibbet. Sycamores survive.
They grow where other trees give up the ghost.
One such, at Craiglockhart, he could recall.
Again he heard the dunnock's douce refrain,
singing for dear life, from lush foliage,
before its notes were silenced, once for all.
Fragments of father's sermon rose to mind -
about The Branch, hope, regeneration.
Now, while still green, a supple slice is bent
into a tongue which will tell of all loss,
tears oozing like resin from a wounded bark:
man and nature in divine harmony.

In Queen's Hall, it will sob and it will sing
of the pity of war - the air fleshily weeping.
And, one being dead, yet will be speaking
through a universal language of peace,
from a pattern once conceived by Gesu.

(The Wilfred Owen violin was made by Steve Burnett, an Edinburgh-based instrument maker. It was produced from a limb of a sycamore tree which grew in the grounds of Craiglockhart Hospital at the time of Owen and Sassoon's fruitful meetings)

WAITING FOR THE WISTARIA

Waiting weeks for wistaria's welter
of tendrils, to titivate Prior's Gate;
to flourish its purple helter-skelter
ear-rings. For Winchester, it seems quite late.
Elsewhere, trailers blossomed against bright brick
facades, yet soon their petals will be spent.
But this one saves its special party trick
till last - like choice Cana wine, heaven scent.

THE SILKSTEAD ROAD

Tramping Yew Hill, thick bluebelled Silkstead Road,
I thought: did monks eye peacock butterflies?
Did they appreciate what Nature showed -
stitchwort, ground ivy, wood anemones?
We took equivocal arrowheads, prised
from the chalk path. I wanted to believe
each blue white flint was pottery disguised;
ancient shards. I so desired to receive
visions of men canopied under trees,
cathedral-vaulted, in tunnelled walkway.
And then thin voices floated on the breeze,
chanting plainsong. Perhaps it was the day,
so clear, that put such notions in my head,
its wildflower profusion, resurrection
in itself. For all we know, the long dead
haunt such paths, offering benediction.

IF FOR A SEASON

Autumnal infernos blaze through The Close.
Crimson creepers lick lintels like tongued flames.
Mellow masonry supports one last rose.
Choristers re-discover conker games.

You can't enjoy such salamandrine shows,
except from your grim ward, through heavy panes.
So many youths ago, Keats waxed verbose
about St. Cross, these misty college lanes.

You yearn for those, but Life has reached the sere,
the burnished leaf, and I suspect you know,
so squeeze your hand and try to transmit cheer.
Your shrivelled face flushes a phoenix glow.

WINCHESTER CATHEDRAL ROOF TOUR

You have to haul yourself up by a rope:

the spiral staircase is so narrow and

the treads so shallow. I don't think you'd cope

right now, but afterwards…

She nods and drinks in my vivid outline

of the tour thirstily. *When I'm quite through*

this chemotherapy; my body's mine

again, we must climb the tower and view

Wolvesey Palace, the Deanery, St. Cross…

Under the heavy wig her eyes burn bright.

I try not to think of her muscle loss,

or that she's shrunk two inches of her height.

All I know is when birds return next spring,

I'll stand on the cathedral roof alone,

or with her. Angels will be hovering,

lest we should dash our feet against a stone.

You cannot see their faces from the ground,

yet worshipful men carved exquisitely

where only God could note, their efforts crowned

in their own hearts.

We know implicitly

that *all over in six months* might mean that:

ambivalence a part of existence.

Magnificat; also requiescat:

twin themes in passionals of persistence.

Now she is confined in the dark stairwells

of pain, where bluebottles accumulate,

but after her suffering has ceased, bells

will peal over pantiles, to celebrate

her courage, endurance and will redound

to those whose vantage point's on higher ground.

CONSTRUCTION (CRUCIFIXION)

All stresses are counterbalanced: cancer,
the carnage of two marriages, cruel death
of her beloved son. Tried in the fire,
forged in the foundry of longsuffering,
three crosses stand against a cedar tree,
which may have sprouted from a mustard seed.
A faceless Christ haloes the deanery.
Meribel Close is stamped with Mondrian's
grid-like shadows and our chequered lives.
Strong shoulders are the lintel of the Door.
Still people pass by on the other side,
embarrassed by their incomprehension;
smelted at the thought of a direct look.
Some gaze at alchemy's transmutation.
The corm of caritas takes root in them.

(Homage To Mondrian by Barbara Hepworth, Winchester Cathedral Close)

SEA CHANGE

Candlelit vigil in Winchester Cathedral

Pilgrims embark, shedding light, to shed light.
We float in dim wickpools. Beneath are depths,
plumbed by past divers, who probed the darkness,
to fix this navicular skeleton,
till all passengers have scaled the gangway.
Hull's expansive ribcage is still on stocks,
uncaulked and so the sea provides the wash
which is empyrean: all height and depth.
We flicker on skystones, below the space
where gopher deck might materialise.
Speleological shipyard of beams,
how can we discern form in your shadows?
Your ark seems empty: no bats or mice squeak
in the black corners where life disappears -
but for uncharted realms of coelacanths.
Footloose, we reach the transept quarterdeck,
where somnolent sailors snooze on stone bunks,
waiting for faded colours to be raised.

Myriads will peer from the multi-decks
and will welcome Love from their balconies.
And now we're in the Captain's gallery,
where He invites voyagers to His table,
to join His golden company. Behind
His gaze stand all His crew, in niche relief,
His figurehead the prow that carves the waves.
Our articles of faith lie in pyxes,
shipwright-wrought, withstanding storms, vortices.
We navigate the bridge by His compass
and try to brave tempestuous elements,
buoyed, anchored by the steerage of our course.
Drowning worlds did not return the raven;
the dove came back, bringing its olive branch
and when it comes again, it will lodge here,
as all restraints are loosed, the vessel launched.

WATTS' MORTUARY CHAPEL

O house of Israel, cannot I do an even more wonderful work with you?

November and blazing beeches burnish
Budburrow Hill. My birthday was this month
and it was on the twentieth we wed.
I did not mind Signor was sixty nine.
He was wary of making the mistake
of marrying a much younger girl -
though I was no virgin Ellen Terry,
but a determined lassie from Loch Ness,
who'd taught clay modelling to tough shoeblacks.
I told him: *Giving ourselves is the one*
necessary gift. So, he acquiesced.
We came to Limnersleave and there he said,
We must build something…I rose with the sun
on the day of consecration and
picked a bunch of white poppies; stood inside.
He puffed up the path, past the Irish yews
into our thoughts, embodied in this form,
through the oak and chestnut door, created

by Compton joiners, with Tau cross hinges:
Passover symbols forged by local smiths.
He marvelled at the moulded angel faces
manufactured by the village children.
The bell in the campanile struck a C:
Be my voice neither feared nor forgotten
was its inscription. Walls' surface shadows
pointed the sorrows and dark side of life.
Perhaps I foreknew that the lachrymals
would contain the oil of joy for mourning
when I placed his ashes in my casket,
here, before the arcuated frontal,
lit by my terracotta candlesticks:
the intimate alongside the sublime.
My glorious prismatic tapestries,
golden corbels and feathered seraphim
revealed all creation as God's garment.
Butterflies emerge from their chrysalis
and a phoenix rises from its embers.
The circle of life is intersected
by the cross of redeeming love. A vine

coils everywhere and we are its branches.
I tried to capture growth/decay; flow/ebb,
to leave a memorial to all those
who perished in The Great War.
Those peacocks did not stand for earthly pride,
but for the hope of immortality.
And now, three hundred yards from the A3,
the tabernacle of the Lord stands firm:
His treasure was in an earthen vessel.
He was the Potter and I was the clay.
See what came from the fiery furnace.

WHITE MARTYRDOM

From Crimthan, sly fox, to Columba,
dove of the church, was a coracle ride
and a conviction that the battle was His.
So the prince swapped his pillow for a stone,
his blackthorn cudgel for an olive branch,
dying daily till oratory steps
were illuminated with a white light.
And he who refused all wool and linen
was comforted by robes of righteousness
for his ultimate peregrination
in the hold of one who calmed the waters
and who was true High King of all Ireland.

(Celtic Christians called a spiritual journey which involved self-sacrifice "white martyrdom")

SESTINA ON SENESCENCE

It comes to all of us - old age -
with aches and pains and memory loss,
which intimate mortality,
reminding us of matters grave:
the inevitable changes;
the unavoidable decline.

Some invitations we now decline.
(Youth does not mix too well with age.)
Our crow's feet presage further changes.
Perhaps our non-attendance is no loss
to those who do not wish to face their grave,
nor trace the lines of their mortality.

Nothing serious in mortality?

And yet Macbeth resisted his decline,

declaiming while one boot was in the grave.

(At least he did not have to reach old age.)

He knew a crown was not worth all the loss.

Sic transit gloria mundi: nothing changes.

Icons who have trounced Life's changes

may rub our noses in mortality.

Though they themselves experienced loss

of face, of friends and suffered love's decline,

they died unwithered by the blasts of age

and somehow made a portal of their grave.

So, do our footsteps all point to the grave?

Does Death's knell merely ring the changes?

Our brain cells burn out from an early age.

Is this how we define mortality:

an inbuilt diminution, a decline?

Or, do we think there's much to gain from loss?

Life's penalty may seem to us a Pyrrhic loss;
we can't resist the pull towards our grave
and feel like Struldbrugs* in our steep decline.
Is entropy to blame for all these changes?
If future medics cure mortality
will we, like Tithonus, just age and age?

Why shun mortality when the changes
need not be loss of anything but age -
the grave not something that we should decline?

**(In Gulliver's Travels, the natives of Luggnagg are immortal, but are, nevertheless, subject to ageing)*